Advance Praise for *12 Steps to Power Presence*

"Great read! In less than an hour you can elevate your leadership game and learn what it takes most leaders a lifetime of leading to understand! *12 Steps to Power Presence* takes 12 books and rolls them into one small book that all healthcare leaders should read."
    —RICK HENVEY, Regional COO, Parkview Health System

"With this brief book, Baldoni brings practical clarity to the often undefined topic of executive presence. He manages to drill deep, while highlighting the absolute essentials along the way. The result is critical reading for anyone who aspires to be in a position of influence . . . and why Baldoni is my favorite writer on the subject of leadership."
    —TIM MORIN, CEO, WJM Associates, Inc.

"So much is written about leadership, but little of it has the direct, practical type of wisdom that leaders (and aspiring leaders) need. John Baldoni's *12 Steps to Power Presence* meets this important need. Leadership of course is more than a job title or the official trappings of power. His discussion of how leaders can use their power in ways that are positive, constructive, and inclusive abounds with important insights and useful suggestions."

    —STEVEN DANIEL, Ph.D., Director of Program Planning,
      The Institute for Management Studies

12 STEPS TO POWER PRESENCE

How to Assert Your Authority to Lead

❖

John Baldoni

AMACOM

AMERICAN MANAGEMENT ASSOCIATION

New York • Atlanta • Brussels • Chicago • Mexico City
San Francisco • Shanghai • Tokyo • Toronto • Washington, D.C.

Bulk discounts available. For details visit:
www.amacombooks.org/go/specialsales
Or contact special sales:
Phone: 800-250-5308
E-mail: specialsls@amanet.org
View all the AMACOM titles at: www.amacombooks.org

This publication is designed to provide accurate and authoritative information in regard to the subject matter covered. It is sold with the understanding that the publisher is not engaged in rendering legal, accounting, or other professional service. If legal advice or other expert assistance is required, the services of a competent professional person should be sought.

Library of Congress Cataloging-in-Publication Data has been applied for and is on record with the Library of Congress.

ISBN–13: 978-0-8144-1691-4
ISBN–10: 0-8144-1691-8

About AMA
American Management Association (www.amanet.org) is a world leader in talent development, advancing the skills of individuals to drive business success. Our mission is to support the goals of individuals and organizations through a complete range of products and services, including classroom and virtual seminars, webcasts, webinars, podcasts, conferences, corporate and government solutions, business books, and research. AMA's approach to improving performance combines experiential learning—learning through doing—with opportunities for ongoing professional growth at every step of one's career journey.

Printing number
10 9 8 7 6 5 4 3 2 1

CONTENTS

American Management Association
www.amanet.org

To leaders who want to make a positive difference.

❖

American Management Association
www.amanet.org

INTRODUCTION

Welcome to *12 Steps to Power Presence!*

12 Steps to Power Presence demonstrates ways managers can improve their presence strategically and tactically to develop the trust of their people so that they can accomplish their goals and the goals of the organization.

There are twelve chapters that will guide you through the process of discovering, developing, and delivering on your leadership presence.

12 Steps to Power Presence explains what it takes to be a leader—one who can develop the trust of people to accomplish individual and organizational goals and results.

Good luck and lead on!

American Management Association
www.amanet.org

WHAT IS LEADERSHIP PRESENCE?

❖

❖

LEADERS PROJECT POWER through their presence.

You can define leadership presence as the presence of authority imbued with a reason to believe. What matters to us most is authenticity. That cannot be faked, but it can be amplified.

Leadership presence is more than style, more than communications. It is the projection of the leader's authentic self. That authenticity is made up of a person's beliefs and convictions and reinforced by behavior. That is, it's not "talking the talk" that matters, it's "walking the walk" that makes the difference. It is what leaders do to convince people to believe in them as people and as leaders.

Leadership presence is the outward manifestation of leadership behavior. While leaders project their leadership, followers authorize it with their approval. Leadership presence is "earned authority." Those two words are important. *Earned* means you have led by example. *Authority* means you have the power to lead others. While organizations confer management roles, it is up to the leader to prove himself or herself by getting others to follow his or her lead. A leader must earn the right to lead others. Title is conferred; leadership is earned.

American Management Association
www.amanet.org

While leaders project power through presence, it is followers who authorize it with their approval.

Consider these examples:

- The plant manager who holds meetings on the shop floor to be close to the work

- The school principal who walks down the hallway greeting by name the children, who grin and send him a cheerful greeting

- The military officer who stays with his troops when the action gets hot and provides a voice of calm when all hell breaks loose

- The coach who shows players how to play the game right and in the process demonstrates what it means to succeed in school and in the community

- The research director who asks questions to stimulate new lines of inquiry and genuinely listens to responses

- The quarterback who steps into the huddle and has every player look to him not only for the play but also for direction

- The mayor who holds weekly meetings with staff directors and encourages them to present their ideas about how best to serve the city

- The CEO who works in an open-plan office and eats in the cafeteria so she can stay in touch with people and listen to their concerns as well as their ideas

You can think of many more examples from your own life. Whichever example you consider, it is important to understand that just as leadership is a reflection of earned authority, leadership presence, which enhances the leadership moment, is derived from the support of others. It cannot be assumed through birth or heritage, though many kings and queens have acted as if they have it and don't. Leadership presence is a form of communication and as such can be taught and put into practice.

Some of us have presence; others must develop it.

Watch how leaders we admire carry themselves. See how they enter a room and engage other people. Look at how they interact with others, both above and below them in rank and authority. Watch how they build coalitions and are able to get things done. Often such leaders are the ones who tackle the impossible tasks and somehow get them done. How? It is because they have created a strong team of people who believe in themselves and their mission and will do whatever it takes to get things done right.

Leadership presence, the power to lead, does not come automatically with rank. While many CEOs and generals may hold heavy titles and their presence may seem lofty, the proof of their leadership is in what they accomplish. People get put into high positions and often don't succeed, a phenomenon documented by Dr. Laurence J. Peter in his 1969 book *The Peter Principle*.[1] Such failures often stem from a lack of leadership presence. These managers fail to build rapport with their people. They assume it is "my way or the highway" and do not accept the counsel or opinions of others.

One of the clearest indicators of leadership presence is the silence that occurs between leader and follower. No pomp. No circumstance. Just being there. This leadership presence occurs on the factory floor when a new hire is schooled by a veteran. You find it on the battlefield in the quiet moments between officers and their troops. And you find it in boardrooms when the CEO has the support of her team. No words are spoken. There is a quiet sense of trust that has developed among all parties.

But here's the key point. While trust is a reciprocal act between leader and follower, it starts with the leader. He must trust his followers by giving them a stake in the enterprise as decision makers and contributors. Followers repay that trust by demonstrating their faith in the leader. That trust contributes to leadership presence in its most pure form and it is something to which all leaders can aspire.

Leadership presence is a powerful attribute of a leader; it amplifies and strengthens a leader's ability to connect with people he or she must lead.[2]

NOTES

1. Laurence J. Peter and Raymond Hull, *The Peter Principle* (New York: William Morrow, 1969).

2. Adapted from John Baldoni, "What Is Leadership Presence?," *HR.com*, June 2007 (used with permission).

CHARACTER COUNTS

❖

❖

ORGANIZATIONS NEED PEOPLE who will stand up for what is right. It sounds so simple, but when organizations come under pressure from competitors, regulators, or market forces, the press for survival becomes paramount. That is why organizations need leaders who are willing to insist on ethical actions in tough times as well as in good times. In truth, most organizations do so; those that do not make headlines. But we can never take such integrity for granted; it must be continually reinforced at every level of the organization. Here are some suggestions for putting character into gear:

♦ *Think character.* Thoughts lay the foundation for action, so when it comes to character you want to be thinking about your role as a leader and how it influences the actions of others. Thinking becomes a preparation for how you will shape the organization. You want to ensure that people you manage as well as those you recruit hold values that complement the vision and mission of your organization. That is, you want people to believe in what your organization does. Character emerges from doing things the right way at the right time. Moral principles should be at the core of your leadership as well as at the core of those you lead.

+ *Communicate character.* Leaders need to speak with integrity. As a leader, what you say matters, so you must carefully choose what you say and how you say it. Speak directly and clearly. Be concise when explaining things. At the same time, be willing to engage in conversations with others. Do not insist on getting in the first word, or the last. Work to make listeners comfortable in having a conversation with you. Good leaders invite feedback, and not just happy talk. They welcome critical conversations in which others are encouraged to speak their minds. Character emanates from your communication, the way you speak as well as the way you listen.

+ *Act on character.* When it comes to character, what you do matters most. It is not good enough to think good thoughts or speak of good intentions; you need to put your intentions into action. You do this through your behavior. You seek to put the needs of the organization first and you act accordingly. You do what the organization needs you to do. In good times, this can be very rewarding because you are doing things that make life better for others: hiring, promoting, and growing the business. In tough times, you are making hard choices about cutting costs, limiting promotions, and even having to let people go.

You can never have too many people of good character. You want to think about ways to perpetuate character throughout your organization. Employees who come into your organization need to strongly manifest an ethical core that governs their behavior. Holding them accountable as you hold yourself accountable ensures that leader and followers are abiding by principles that truly mean something.

You reinforce character through organizational values. If you want people to treat others with respect, that is, tolerate alternative points of view, insist on honesty in all actions, and be transparent in their motives, then you write these values down and insist that everyone abide by them. Beginning of course with yourself.

Another way of thinking of character as it applies to presence is as a foundation for your brand. Every successful product projects characteristics that consumers find appealing. The same goes for your character. Presence, when rooted in the authentic leadership self, is a demonstration of integrity that encourages others to follow your lead. Why? Because they consider you the real deal, a person of good character.

FIVE ATTRIBUTES OF AUTHORITY

❖

American Management Association
www.amanet.org

❖

AUTHORITY DOES COME FROM TITLE, but it is earned through actions. Inept executives fritter away their authority by their behavior, taking the counsel of none but themselves and failing to listen and learn from others. Authority is what holds leadership promise together. With it, you can lead; without it, you might as well do something else.

Many leaders come to authority naturally; they embrace it totally and wield it like a sword to demonstrate their power. Others adopt it reluctantly, seemingly shirking from the responsibility. In truth, neither approach is wholly right nor wholly wrong. Leaders must embrace command, but they must recognize that their power stems from the people they lead.

There are five attributes of authority as it applies to leadership:

1. *Decisiveness.* Leaders need to exert their ideas. No Hamlets ("To be or not to be") wanted. The ability to make tough decisions is crucial to a leader's ability to lead. We remember General Dwight D. Eisenhower making the decision to launch a full frontal assault of the Normandy coast on D-Day. His final decision was short and to the point: "Okay, we'll go."[1] But the decision was the culmination of years of military buildup

of men and material as well as days of deliberation over weather conditions. By contrast, another former general, Alexander Haig, serving as secretary of state, jumped to a press podium in the White House on the day in March 1981 when President Ronald Reagan was shot and exclaimed, "I am in control here, in the White House."[2] Bad move. The vice president, the speaker of the house, and president pro temporare of the Senate were very much alive and, according to the Constitution, ahead of him as potential successors. Rash decision making can be disastrous. You can take time to consider the options and deliberate the conditions and consequences, but ultimately you must pull the trigger on the decision. I will talk more about decisiveness later in Step 5.

2. *Accomplishment.* Leaders must, plain and simple, get things done. We want our leaders to do what they tell us they will do. When the CEO of a public company promises a new product or service as well as increased earnings and profits, he must deliver. Otherwise we tend to doubt his sincerity. Is he preening for the cameras? Is he angling for another job? Or is he clueless as to the real situation? Some executives are notorious for blue-sky predictions about production and revenues. All too often the situation changes and they end up with egg on their faces. Contrast their dismal performance with that of executives who know how to mastermind a turnaround. Very often by working together with the existing employees, these executives can right the ship by reducing debt, cutting costs, and improving earnings. Getting things done is essential to authority; it the raison d'être of leadership.

3. *Persuasiveness.* Operating in a vacuum—or in a closed office—does not a leader make. No leader of an enterprise larger than a three-person operation can do much by himself. Sometimes autocratic executives will get into trouble because their heavy-handed management style turns people off. Then when the heat is on and they need the support of others, they will often find no one standing behind them. All leaders need the cooperation and collaboration of others. Therefore, leaders must bring others to the cause; that's a key measure of leadership. Essential to that mantra is an ability to communicate the objectives in ways that encourage people to buy into the process. You need to make the objective not only tangible but possible, as well as good for the enterprise. Some tasks are onerous—layoffs, closures, and terminations—but if they are done for the good of the organization, and ultimately the people in it, then they must be done. It is up to the leader to make the case.

4. *Courage.* Leaders must hold to the power of their beliefs and convictions, provided they are ethical, honest, and in keeping with organizational goals and beliefs. Standing up to bully bosses requires guts. Standing up to shareholders who want job cuts for short-term profits also takes guts. Standing up to public perceptions that seem reasonable but are unrealistic and uninformed also requires a measure of guts. But courage is essential to leadership. We know well the stories of soldiers in the field who perform acts of heroism to save their buddies. What we do not know so well is the courage all soldiers display when they go out on dangerous missions day after day. Police officers and firefighters, too, put themselves in harm's way regularly. Similarly, people

in business demonstrate courage by blowing the whistle on illegalities or standing up for a fellow worker who is being harassed. Some even question the ideas of a senior leader. We do not celebrate courage enough in our corporate culture, but we should because it can be the backbone that individuals need to stand up for themselves and their beliefs. As Tadashi Kume, former executive of Honda Motor Company, once said, "I tell people that if the [company] president says a crow is white, you have to argue that a crow is really black."[3]

5. *Inspiration.* Ever look up in the sky at night and see the moon on a crisp, clear night and wonder what it was like up there? Mankind has been doing that for time immemorial. In 1969 that look skyward became reality for two astronauts who set foot on the moon. Ten more astronauts followed their steps in subsequent years. Their quest inspired a nation and along the way revolutionized computer technology as well as many other things. Entrepreneurial ventures have something of a moon-shot quality to them. These ventures, be it a new software company or a technology outfitter or a service provider, require a healthy dose of dreaming to succeed. People who work for those ventures feel jazzed when they come to work; they are inspired by doing something new, different, and beneficial for their customers and themselves. All of us want to belong to something greater than ourselves, and inspiration is essential. Authority coupled with a sense of aspiration bonds people to the leader.

Decisiveness. Accomplishment. Persuasiveness. Courage. Inspiration. These attributes reinforce your authority to lead.

While authority is essential to leadership, it does not come automatically with rank or position. Authority, like trust, must be earned, but here's the difference. Trust requires time to develop. Authority, especially in most hierarchies, is assumed. People will grant you permission to lead. They want you to lead; they want you to succeed. Why? Because your followers have a vested interest in the organization; your leadership is vital to their success. That said, authority can be lost. Before that happens, it is important to understand the nature of authority and how it develops.

NOTES

1. David Eisenhower, *Eisenhower at War, 1943–1945* (New York: Random House, 1987), p. 251.

2. Tim Weiner, "Alexander M. Haig, Jr., Forceful Aide to 2 Presidents, Dies," *New York Times,* February 21, 2010.

3. Susan Chira, "Honda Is Powered by Risks," *New York Times,* June 15, 1987.

American Management Association
www.amanet.org

LEVERAGING POWER

❖

American Management Association
www.amanet.org

❖

OUR SOCIETY IS KNEE-DEEP IN PEOPLE who misuse power. While their aims are often selfish, as we have seen with managers at corrupt companies, their power is nonetheless substantial; they hurt people purposefully and maliciously. Such managers in those organizations use power as a weapon; it becomes their means to a selfish end. Much of their motivation derives from greed, but in some cases, abuses of power come from ignorance. They simply never cared to learn how to use power appropriately.

Power is intrinsic to leadership presence, so it is important to discover ways to use it positively. You must learn to apply it in the workplace in order to create allies, lead others, and achieve sustainable results.

Here are four things you need to know about power:

1. *Find power.* When you want to get things done, be it a change initiative or a special project, you need to find people who will give you the support (and funding) you need to get started. That support often, but not always, comes from people at the top; they have the power. Identify who can help you and go after them. You need to develop a business case to support your initiative. Your case should address the benefits to

stakeholders (customers, employees, shareholders) as well as to the bottom line. And your business case will not suffer if you mention how it will benefit those at the top, by demonstrating either their farsightedness or the improvement to the bottom line.

2. *Demonstrate power.* In the heyday of the Roman Empire, its disciplined legions were the manifestation of Roman power. Military prowess alone, however, did not hold the empire together. It ensured the peace so that the Roman system that fostered commerce, trade, building, and education could proliferate. The lesson is that power is more than force of might. It is the authority to make good things happen. When you have power, use it to further the aims of the organization, not simply your own agenda. For managers, it means using power to achieve results. Marshal resources to develop a new project and bring it home on time and on budget.

3. *Share power.* All good managers know that power without the support of others is useless. The irony of power is that it can never be wholly centralized. Certainly in dictatorships, power emanates from the person at the top, but he is supported by legions of minions who are only too happy to carry out his whims. Why? Because they receive some kind of benefit, either personally or for their families. Within the corporate sector, the CEO is the person in charge, but successful business leaders delegate, delegate, delegate. And with authority, too. One of the secrets to Warren Buffett's success is his willingness to let managers manage. Berkshire Hathaway is a holding company; its portfolio of companies is largely self-managed. Buffett provides

advice and counsel as well as some funding, but the running of the company is left to the senior leadership team. That's a genuine power share.

4. *Influence power.* Sales professionals soon learn that often their best way to make a sale is to gain the support of the recommender, or person of influence. Winning that person to your side is often the most effective way to make a sale. This is because the decision maker will often look to the recommender and concur with her decision. For managers, influence is the chief way things get done in a large organization, particularly when implementing processes across functions. A manager in charge has no direct authority over the person he is asking to change; what he possesses is the power of his ideas as well as his powers of persuasion.

Are there limits to power? Of course.

Those who crave power will not be in a mood to share. Absolute power, as the adage goes, corrupts absolutely. Those who put themselves first—be it a despot or a bully boss—will never ever share. In the case of despots, you need to depose them; in the case of bullies, you need to boot them. Few are worthy of rehabilitation. Power for them is both a means to an end as well as the end itself. While that is reality, managers should not shy away from leveraging power nor should they shy away from sharing it. Power is essential to presence and in turn vital to leadership.

American Management Association
www.amanet.org

BE DECISIVE

❖

❖

DECISIONS ARE WHAT DEFINE A LEADER.

One CEO I interviewed said that you need leaders only for the big decisions that affected the organization as a whole. Every other kind of decision should be decided by people closest to the consequences of that decision. Ritz-Carlton puts this into practice by having its front-line staff do whatever is practical to fulfill their customer service commitment without additional charge to the customer and without soliciting permission from their supervisors. Customer convenience and satisfaction comes first.

Front-line decision making also gives hourly workers in manufacturing plants the authority to stop the production line if they think something is wrong. Likewise, many companies grant customer service representatives a degree of autonomy within a certain dollar amount to make decisions that will resolve consumer complaints. As a result, customers may receive a replacement product or full reimbursement.

These examples place decision making in its rightful context. The criterion for making decisions within a business environment should be the effect the decision has on the company's value equation as it relates to customers, employees, and shareholders. The value equation includes more than good financials, although good returns are essential. Value encompasses more of what many refer to as the "triple bottom line," which defines how well a company delivers on its economic, social, and environmental commitments.

Considering a triple bottom line gives managers the freedom as well as the challenge of considering how their decisions will affect customers, employees, shareholders, and the community. By considering the value proposition, you anchor the decision in reality and you also do something else: You challenge employees to think outside of themselves to the consequences of their decisions. Too much consideration can lead to "analysis paralysis," but enough consideration can be nurtured by the manager through ongoing communications. Here are some suggestions:

- *Seek input.* Decisions may be and often are made from the gut. Design decisions on everything from automobiles to kitchenware are based upon instinct, but it is good to balance your gut with ideas gained from consumer research as well as from others the team. Yet too much data can not only shake a hard drive, it can also make for fuzzy decision making. Where possible, ask for recommendations from the team; ask them what they think. You can decide by consensus or on your instinct, but at least you will have brought other thinking into the decision mix.

- *Ask questions.* One technique for soliciting input is to ask questions. But good questions are more than simple requests for more information. Questions may provoke awareness that more thinking is required. Ruminative thinking may delay a decision process temporarily, but the questions raised and the answers provoked may guide the manager and her team to make a better decision. You can also use questions to challenge conventional thought in ways that force people to look at their situation in a new and different light.

- *Decide.* Absolutely! The purpose of decision making is to make a decision, that is, to come to a conclusion and proceed. Too often we may postpone the process hoping a situation will go away. That's wishful thinking. So, after you've studied, debated, and conversed, pull the trigger. Make the decision and stand up for it. Do not seek to make a decision an orphan. Make certain you communicate your reasons, especially if the topic is controversial. If you stand tall and show that you can take the heat, you may not gain points for the decision, but you will gain respect for your convictions.

Try as we might, it is inevitable that we will make wrong choices that lead to wrongheaded decisions. Decision making is rooted in accountability, even when the outcome is less than desirable. The hope is that the consequences of poor decisions can be reversed. And in many instances they can by applying some of the same communications lessons, such as asking questions, listening to evaluations, and seeking to make amends as swiftly as possible. Sometimes simply accepting responsibility for a poor decision is enough; other times you need to make an effort to right the wrongs, particularly when they involve customers or employees.

The decisions a leader makes today will define her legacy for tomorrow. But if such a leader is taught to make good decisions in a way that facilitates two-way communication, she will have a proper framework for making good decisions. She will have the communication skills necessary to ask for input and assistance as well as the confidence to know that she can make the right decision. After all, as Winston Churchill put it, "The price of greatness is responsibility."[1]

NOTE

1. Winston Churchill, Address at Harvard University, September 6, 1943.

American Management Association
www.amanet.org

BE STRAIGHT WITH PEOPLE

❖

❖

ONE OF THE BEST STARTING POINTS for developing your leadership message is asking yourself, "What do people expect to hear?" It is also one of the worst places to start. Let me explain. Feeding the audience's expectations is fun; it's like throwing peanuts to monkeys. Telling people what they want to hear is the staple of politicians. Audiences love it when politicians promise better roads, better schools, and better health care. But skeptics, typically from the other party, ask, "Who's going to pay for it?" The taxpayer of course!

YOUR MESSAGE GOES HERE

So a speaker must be honest with his audience. If you promise more government, you must show how you will pay for it. Otherwise you lose credibility. Likewise, if you promise lower taxes, discuss the services that will be discontinued. Ultimately credibility is a public speaker's stock in trade. Therefore, it is imperative that the leader talk about what he needs to say and frame it within the context of what the organization needs.

That's why asking "what does the audience want to hear?" is good for generating ideas but bad for framing an argument. Audiences are owed straight talk. This is especially true when executives are speaking to their employees.

One of the toughest speeches any leader will have to give is the announcement of a plant closing or a big layoff. One friend of mine in the pharmaceutical industry has done it half a dozen times or so, and he swears it never gets any easier. Telling the audience what they want to hear would be to say, "We're closing, but you've all got job security." Instead, the leader might have to say, "We're closing and we are able to keep some, but not all, of you. Here's our plan for going forward." Tough, you bet. Honest, absolutely.

Transforming a message from what the audience wants to hear into what the audience needs to hear is critical to a leader's credibility. Pandering to an audience's base needs is akin to a "buy one get one free" coupon: It satisfies an immediate need but does not build brand loyalty. No one welcomes bad news, but they may need to hear it. The same applies to speakers. If you only talk up the good stuff and avoid the truth, you are quickly branded as a phony. So for your next presentation on a tough topic, here are some suggestions:

+ *Slay the dragon.* Acknowledge the big issue. For example, if the plant is to be closed, announce it early in your presentation. Do not leave the audience hanging. At the same time, if the future of the plant is in doubt, address the issue before you talk about anything else. Speakers often make the mistake of trying to avoid the issue by assuming (falsely) that audiences do not need to know. Wrong. People always frame whatever they hear in terms of "what's in it for me." So even if your presentation is not about a big issue, if it is on people's minds, you must acknowledge it. Otherwise listeners will be waiting for the shoe to drop. So get it out of the way immediately, and then move forward.

◆ *Make the case.* If you are the bearer of bad news, talk about why you or your team made the decision. Use facts, not opinions. Talk about market conditions as well as prospects for growth. For example, if your business model is uncompetitive, propose ways to reduce costs as well as innovate. Be as specific as possible by telling employees what you expect of them.

◆ *Offer redemption.* When people are losing something— an opportunity, a promotion, or a job—they go into a kind of shock. Very little of what you say next will have any effect. So here's where the human side comes in. For example, announcements of head count reduction are often coupled with offers of jobs in other cities, transition coaching, or job retraining. Compensation packages may also be disclosed. People may not hear these offerings immediately, but you must announce them, as well as pass out handouts with the offerings.

EMPATHY MATTERS

How you deliver the message counts. The tougher the message, the more resolute yet more human the leader must be. You demonstrate resolve when announcing a cutback, addressing product failure, or a revealing a corporate reorganization. You demonstrate humanity when you acknowledge the difficulty of the message but acknowledge the pain that it may cause others. By showing empathy for those adversely affected by the decision, the leader shows compassion and understanding. Stories describing the care that went into the decision coupled with the realization of the hardship the decision would create puts a human face on what might be perceived as a simple dollars-and-cents equation.

No one likes to deliver a tough message, but doing so builds a foundation for mutual trust. Audiences may not like what they hear, but they will, at least subconsciously, credit the speaker for being straight. There is so much hype and hoopla in the world that talking straight actually cuts through the clutter. People remember your honesty. So, if you have to deliver a tough speech, embrace the opportunity. It may sting for the moment, but over time the sting goes away and you are recognized for what you are: a straight talker.

APPEARANCE DOES MATTER

❖

❖

IF YOU START WITH THE PREMISE that leadership is about results and results ultimately come from the cooperation and collaboration of others, then it makes more and more sense that leadership is less about the leader and more about the followers. No leader can achieve anything by herself; she does it by working with others to achieve intended goals.

Therefore, anything you can do to positively affect the relationship between leader and follower is critically important. And that includes how you look. You must project authority and look like you are in command. How you look is vitally important. Here are some things to keep in mind when presenting yourself as a leader:

- ◆ *Invest in your appearance.* Take a long look at yourself in the mirror. Women and men do this differently. Women, I'm convinced, look in the mirror to see their flaws; men I know look in the mirror to admire themselves. Women gain a pound and see themselves as rotund; men see an expanding waistline as normal, or perhaps as an example of clothes that have shrunk in the wash. An exaggeration, yes, but women know better than men that appearances matter. If you expect people to follow you, give them reasons to follow your lead. Groom yourself. Dress neatly and smartly. Also take care of what's inside you. Good diet and healthy exercise are important to your looks as well as your health.

◆ *Watch your expressions.* For leaders, the adage that the face is a mirror to the soul has validity. If you frown frequently, or reply with a snarl, people will avoid you. Why? Because they assume one of two things: one, you don't want to be bothered, or two, you want to bite someone's head off, perhaps theirs. Often leaders have no idea how they look until someone, like an executive coach or a trusted advisor, pulls them aside. So lighten up. Before an important meeting, sit down, think a calming thought, and, yes, check yourself in the mirror. Smile. It will reduce the tension in your face.

◆ *Radiate authority.* When Ronald Reagan walked into the room, heads turned and people gravitated to him. He had the movie star appeal; so too did John Kennedy. At the same time, Reagan in particular looked the part, but he was approachable. He was a superb storyteller as well as a good listener.

Attentive listening, or what we call active listening, is a powerful way to make a connection with another individual. When done purposefully and intently, it communicates a concern for others and reflects the listener's authenticity. It is more than charisma, a form of radiant charm; leadership listening is an ability to put yourself in another person's shoes and make that person feel as if he or she is the most important person in the room.

Watch your CEO stride through the workplace; if she pauses to chat with people and really listens, she is someone to follow. If she blows by with a faux wave or cursory glance (and assuming she is not running for a plane), chances are that person is more concerned with herself than with others and as a result may not be liked or respected; she could be moving on soon.

The way you present yourself as a leader is critical. It affects your ability to connect in a way that is authentic and leads people to give you the benefit of the doubt. Every leader must earn trust, but the door to trust can be opened only if people are willing to give you a second look, or better yet a long look and a good listen. That is why appearances matter. So yes, go ahead and buy that new suit; if it makes you feel more in control and in command then by all means go for it. But keep in mind that what's inside the suit matters more. You learned that in elementary school in the story of the emperor's new clothes, but it never hurts to repeat it. And don't forget to smile once in a while too.[1]

NOTE

1. Adapted from John Baldoni, "Appearance Does Matter," Darwin Online/CXO Media, June 30, 2005 (used with permission).

STEP 8

INSTILL PRIDE OF PURPOSE

❖

❖

IF YOU INTEND TO LEAD OTHERS, you need to give them not only reasons to follow you, but also reasons to be part of your organization. Often a sense of belonging comes down to feeling good about what you do as well as how you do it. Call it pride of purpose.

Every manager should want his employees to manifest similar pride, but reality tells us that this occurs all too infrequently. So the challenge for managers becomes how to instill genuine pride in the team so that employees feel proud of what they do and the company for which they work.

Instilling such pride is never easy. Real pride is not happy talk; it is pride centered on purpose. Employees who love what they do and the organization to which they belong demonstrate their support for their organization in words but most especially in actions. They do whatever is necessary to get the job done and done right. That is the kind of pride every employer should strive to engender.

Managers seeking to instill such pride need to ask three crucial questions:

HOW WELL DO MY EMPLOYEES UNDERSTAND WHAT IS EXPECTED OF THEM?

Most companies do an excellent job of defining tasks but sometimes fall short when explicating roles and responsibilities. When this occurs, employees may not know who does what or why. This is how things fall through the cracks, leaving bosses and employees scrambling to make do with last-minute changes.

Good managers make certain their people know not only their own jobs but everyone else's too. Such managers also encourage others to pitch in when their work slackens and another teammate's increases.

HOW WELL DO MY EMPLOYEES KNOW HOW THEIR WORK COMPLEMENTS THE GREATER WHOLE?

Companies often do not take enough time to compliment their people for a good job. Worse, they fail to demonstrate how employees' contributions help the company succeed. Therefore, it falls to the manager to create the links that show how what someone does in purchasing improves quality of products, how an accountant ensures a more robust bottom line, or how a customer service representative builds loyalty with customers. These tasks, and so many more, are important to corporate success.

WHAT CAN I DO TO FOSTER MORE PRIDE?

Company mission statements that recognize employee value are worthwhile, but it is the manager who brings them alive. This is where the manager praises from the front. Successful managers I know make a habit of acknowledging accomplishments of individuals in front of the team. These managers make it clear that team success relies upon individual contributions.

Now comes the tough part. The answers to these questions will likely mean the manager will have to do more. This is the part of management that requires leadership, the willingness to do what is necessary to help the team become more productive, and by extension more aware of their personal contributions. When they do, pride ensues.

Pride is essential; we want our employees to express it, but as with all things prideful, too much of it can be onerous. We call that arrogance—it turns people off. Organizations that manifest arrogance get into trouble because they overlook issues, ignore customer concerns, and even alienate employees.

Pride, on the other hand, turns people on, and that is what we want to encourage. Pride in the work is essential to fostering a more energized workplace. And when employees feel such energy they are more likely to want to come to work and do a good job. Morale improves, too, and few workplaces can do without a strong team spirit.

American Management Association
www.amanet.org

TO LEAD IS TO ASSERT

❖

American Management Association
www.amanet.org

❖

ANY DISCUSSION OF LEADERSHIP presence brings up the topic of assertiveness. For the past few decades, assertiveness training has been a popular subject for people interested in improving their opportunities for career advancement. While the topic seems less popular than in years past, the concept of elevating your profile through words and actions is a sound one. It is particularly relevant for leaders. No leader can be shy and retiring in an organizational setting. A leader must be out in front, fully engaged with her team.

Assertiveness is essential and there are ways to demonstrate it.

- *Demonstrate self-confidence.* The root of leadership assertiveness must be belief in one's own abilities. That does not mean you feel you can take on any challenge any time. That's not confidence, that's stupidity. Self-confidence is the belief that you can tackle a challenge because you have the skills and abilities. Self-confidence also means you have enough belief in yourself to ask for help if things take a turn for the worse. Failure to ask for help is a shortcoming.

- *Volunteer.* Managers love it when people step forward to assume responsibility. It makes their job so much easier.

It is essential that leaders demonstrate that they are willing to take on new assignments, especially onerous ones. Such volunteerism for a good cause encourages others to step forward too.

◆ *Honor the team.* When speaking about the work, make certain that people know you value their contributions. Leaders who put their people first are those who gain the most followers. By asserting the specific talents and skills of individuals on the team, you demonstrate that you understand how teams function. It also makes people want to follow their leader. That in itself is another form of confidence.

Sometimes the call to assert yourself stems from the situation. The leader steps forward to assume a task, but the assertiveness is applicable to getting the job done. For example, if a company needs someone to head up a new process initiative, stepping forward to assume that task demonstrates that you are willing to assume responsibility.

Enlisting others to work on the project, however, will require less assertiveness and more persuasion. You will need to sell the benefits of working on the project, particularly if the deadline is tight and the hours will be long. Managers, of course, can require people to work on it, and that's what often happens, but to accomplish something lasting you want to treat your people as volunteers. That is, you have to engage their hearts and minds.

Assert the benefits of the work by demonstrating what the job entails, the skills necessary, and the challenges of working as a team on something new, different, and integral to the success of the organization.

PROJECTING HOPE AND OPTIMISM

❖

American Management Association
www.amanet.org

❖

HOPE IS ESSENTIAL to the leadership process. Leaders must instill hope in their people by communicating its importance in thought, word, and deed. Hope is essential to outcome—to obtaining results. Without hope, no officer could send a soldier into battle, no coach could field a team, and no manager could expect to complete a project. Communication is essential to hope because communication is how hope is transmitted from leader to follower.

It is essential to define hope. Let's start with what hope is not. Hope is not the feeling that everything will be okay no matter what happens. That of kind of thinking leads people to jump off cliffs with homemade wings in the *hope* they might fly. Instead, genuine hope is a sense of optimism that, despite the odds, their individual contributions matter and do make a positive difference.

The medical analogy is this: A physician treating a patient with a terminal condition will not cure the patient, but if the patient believes in the therapy and the physician, the months or years remaining can be better than they would be without hope. By the same token, when leaders ask their people to do what seems impossible, it can often be achieved because the followers have faith in the leader and hope in their own abilities.

Entrepreneurs trade in hope; they have ideas for new products or services but need capital and people to move from ideation to production. That requires hope. Not simply hope, but a sense that what they do makes a real difference if they have the right resources and the right people. Since hope is essential to effective leadership, here are three ideas that managers can use to communicate its necessity:

1. *Project optimism.* Yes, work is hard and sometimes tedious, but managers can do something about it. First, they must talk up the benefits of the work; for example, discuss how the team's efforts will enable the company to turn a profit and keep people employed. Second, managers can address ways to improve the work and find ways to do so. Third, managers can lighten up. Those in charge who crack jokes at their own expense or smile at people when they meet them project a positive attitude. Few of us can be upbeat all the time, but if you make an attempt at lightness, people will respond positively. Such attitudes are not only healthy for the team, they are contagious; others will emulate your example.

   Hope flourishes on the notion that things can be better. The net result of any work should be improvement, either a correction or a new way of doing things. Otherwise it is friction, a drag on the enterprise. We have likely had the unfortunate experience of working on projects that have gone sour, and working on them is akin to playing out the clock in a basketball game when you are behind by fifty points. By contrast, imagine the sense of exhilaration that floods over a team when what it is working on—a process, a therapy, a piece of software code—will improve things for someone else.

Leaders need to communicate that optimism to the entire team; it is uplifting and creates momentum that carries through the project.

2. *Tell the truth.* Unwarranted optimism, however, can be fatal. That is why leaders owe the truth to their people. When things turn bad, leaders must be honest and straightforward. No one likes to give or receive bad news, but withholding bad news is a luxury no leader can afford. And while it may seem that truth, especially if it is bad, is antithetical to hope, the opposite is true. Withholding bad news will instill false hope, and when the truth is later revealed, the bond between leader and follower is ruptured, sometimes forever. But if you are up-front and truthful, you create a basis upon which you can build a strategy and develop tactics to achieve a goal. That action instills hope.

3. *Demonstrate resilience.* Few things in leadership, as in life, go as planned. Setbacks are inevitable in every endeavor, be it academics, sports, or business. Engineers are often the most resilient of folks; as ones who diagnose causes of failure, discover possible remedies, and implement solutions, they are accustomed to trying option after option in the quest for a viable solution. Setbacks do not deter them, so much so that they often must be pulled off projects, or at least persuaded to implement less-than-optimum solutions, just to keep things moving. In short, they have resiliency, honed by their knowledge and skills and nurtured by their hope of improvement.

Hope is not the "be all end all." Gordon Sullivan, former U.S. Army chief of staff, co-authored an insightful book, *Hope Is Not a Method,* about how the U.S. Army transformed itself from an organization of draftees into an all-volunteer force, in part by adopting and implementing principles of organizational learning. Leaders, according to Sullivan, do not *hope* for change, they make change by focusing on needs and developing strategies that will improve organizational effectiveness. In other words, you must not simply hope, you must act.[1]

Action, of course, is integral to effective leadership. And when you couple that with a sense of optimism tempered by reality, you create conditions for people to hope. Hope is essential to results, whether you are developing a new system or reorganizing a department. People doing the work must have the sense that what they do matters and will make things better for individuals and the organization. Without hope we are lost; with hope we can achieve. Hope may not be a "method," but it certainly is the spirit that keeps us going.[2]

NOTES

1. Gordon Sullivan and Michael Harper, *Hope Is Not a Method* (New York: Times Books, 1996).

2. Adapted from John Baldoni, "Opting for Optimism," Darwin Online/CXO Media, September 2004 (used with permission).

COACHING YOUR BOSS

❖

❖

SOME OF MANAGING UP involves coaching. While coaching is typically given from manager to employer, the reverse can occur. Just as you strive to manage expectations, you can strive to manage feedback. Bosses deserve feedback from employees too. Many bosses may not realize this, but a self-motivated, leadership-oriented employee can advise them. The first rule in giving feedback is trust. Managers must make it safe for their employees; that is, they cannot exact repercussions for telling the truth. This is easier said than done. But if you have built a level of trust with your boss, and you do this by doing your job and performing well, you have earned the right to give feedback.

Feedback is an essential first step in coaching. Your honesty will be invaluable. So many leaders complain that they do not know what is going on in their organization because people do not tell them. Well, the blame lies partly with the leader for not asking, but it also is up to employees to be forthcoming. Upward coaching is seldom formal; it is usually in the form of a conversation. Here are some things to observe:

- *Open with a positive.* Compliment the boss on what she is doing well. For example, discuss how the boss is managing a project or interacting with employees. Create a foundation for the discussion to proceed on a constructive basis.

- *Give honest feedback from peers.* Be straight and tell the boss how he is doing. Do not sugarcoat. You can be diplomatic, but play it straight. If the boss is letting deadlines slip, tell him. If the boss is too hard on an employee without cause, say something. If the boss is overlooking issues, raise those issues. As an employee you also can tell the boss how he is relating to your peers. Every manager needs to know this; getting the work done depends upon the relationship between boss and employee. Your insight into this aspect of management is vital.

- *Offer assistance.* Your candor lays the groundwork for your support. If there are issues, provide your help. Volunteer for an assignment. Offer to be a team leader. Serve as a liaison between the boss and your team, but be careful not to be a mediator. You cannot solve issues between boss and employees, you can only advise. If you get sucked into such situations, back off. On the other hand, as an honest broker between boss and employee, you can provide insight to both sides.

Coaching your boss is a leadership behavior. It demonstrates that you believe in yourself and are motivated to make a positive difference. Such coaching emerges from your relationship with the boss that is founded upon performance. You cannot coach if you do not deliver. Therefore, the key to managing upward is understanding the boss, followed by action. Get to know what needs doing, and then do it, and make yourself available to do more. Do not become overextended. Pick your spots. That is, volunteer for activities that make a positive difference and add value to the enterprise. This means you must ration your time and energy. This, too, is a good thing; it emerges from your personal discipline and your motivation to excel.

PROMOTE YOURSELF

❖

American Management Association
www.amanet.org

❖

EVER WONDER WHY JERKS GET PROMOTED and good guys get left behind?

That's a question that resonates around the proverbial water-cooler and one I've often heard in one form or another in my executive coaching. You most often hear it when someone people really dislike gets promoted. Often that person is someone who looks good, presents well, and may be something of a kiss-up. The manager everyone likes, or thinks could do a better job, is left behind. So why is that? Well one reason is because the manager who is perceived to be good is leading down, but not up, while the person who is promoted is doing more leading up. In reality, the empty-suit executive is not truly leading; he's merely showing off. The better manager is leading, but not doing a good job of impressing his bosses. And that can be a problem come promotion time.

One of the most common things holding good people back is an inability to demonstrate their competence. They are perceived to lack leadership presence; that is, they do not inspire confidence upward or give more senior managers a reason to believe in their leadership. Sometimes effective leaders are very good at guiding their teams but not very good at shining their leadership star. They are so focused on doing the work as well as empowering others that they overlook opportunities to shine themselves. Is shining yourself necessary? In our management culture, absolutely. Here are some ways to augment your leadership brand:

- ◆ *Be the one.* Do your job first and foremost. You have to be good at what you do by meeting and exceeding your objectives. Specifically, good leaders enable others to do the real work; the leader plays the supporting role. Show-offs may micromanage if the big boss is watching but disappear when there is real work to be done. They spend more time schmoozing with the bosses than providing direction and support for their teams.

- ◆ *Demonstrate initiative.* Volunteer for the tough assignments. Make it known that when problems arise, you want to be the one to troubleshoot. One differentiator between the empty-suit executive and the good leader is competence. Show-offs flounder when the heat is on; leaders simply get on with the job and, most important, bring others to the cause.

- ◆ *Show off.* We live in a celebrity-driven culture. As obnoxious as that may be, some celebs can teach leaders a thing or two about getting noticed. Dress well. Socialize appropriately. At the same time, unlike celebrities, be courteous to all and acknowledge your team. One of the best ways to brag is to talk up the accomplishments of your team. Your team is a reflection of your leadership style; their achievements are a reflection of your ability to get things done right.

No amount of polishing will make an empty-suit manager a good leader. In fact, one reason why there are levels of incompetence in management is because people have been promoted to positions over their heads. It is the Peter Principle, yes, but it is really the fault of senior management for not doing enough due diligence on whom they promote.

Decision makers allow themselves to be dazzled by a sharp dresser and a good talker rather than asking questions of people who work for the empty-suit executive. Dialogues with direct reports would reveal that the person does not really know his stuff, does not set good direction, and does not inspire trust and confidence in others.

Grousing about incompetent people getting promoted is not the answer. If you want to move up, you need to demonstrate the things necessary to impress others. You need to radiate confidence as well as maintain composure. You also need to make it known that you are ready and willing to tackle new challenges. Doing these things takes time, but when they are performed diligently and with a little style, you will be noticed and even promoted.

In short, you need to leverage your leadership presence to make yourself known, your influence felt, and your results count. When these things happen you will be fulfilling your leadership potential and becoming the leader that your team needs you to be.

Lead on!

INDEX

ABOUT THE AUTHOR

JOHN BALDONI is an internationally recognized leadership development consultant, speaker, and author of many books, including *Lead Your Boss* and *Lead by Example*. In 2010 he was ranked number 12 on the list of the "30 Most Influential Leadership Gurus" by www.LeadershipGurus.net. John is a regular contributor to the online sites of *Business Week*, *Fast Company*, *Harvard Business Review*, and the *Washington Post*. He has been featured or quoted in numerous publications including the *New York Times*, *USA Today*, and *Investor's Business Daily*. His leadership resource website is www.johnbaldoni.com.

American Management Association
www.amanet.org